This book belongs to :

BAIGANI

EGGPLANT

SILA

CORN

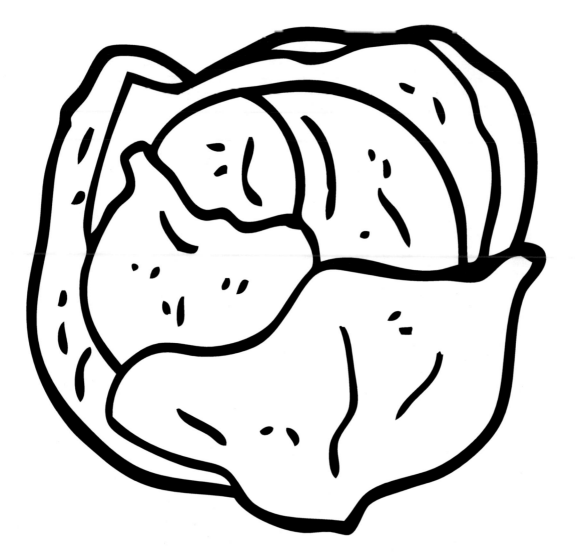

KAVETI

CABBAGE

UTO

BREADFRUIT

JAINA

BANANA

DALO

TARO

NIU
COCONUT

VARASA
ONION

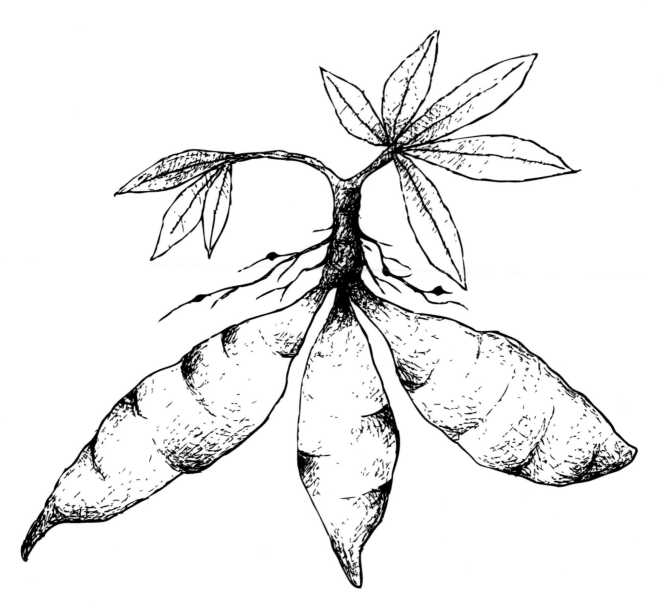

TAVIOKA
CASSAVA

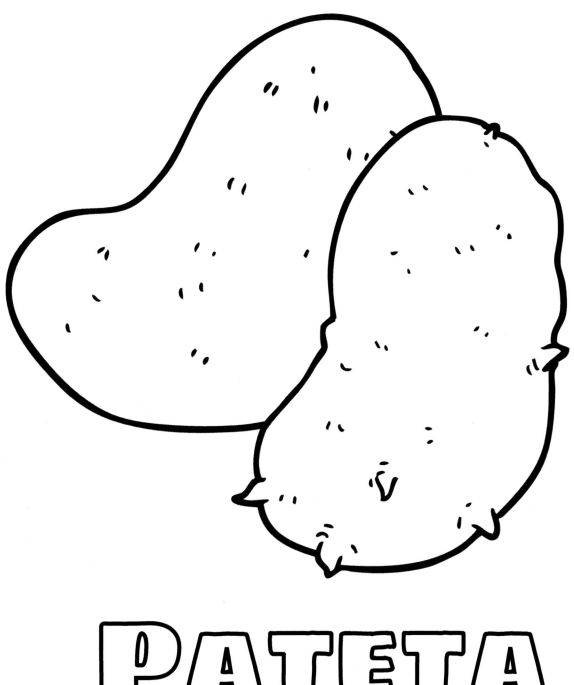

PATETA

PATATO

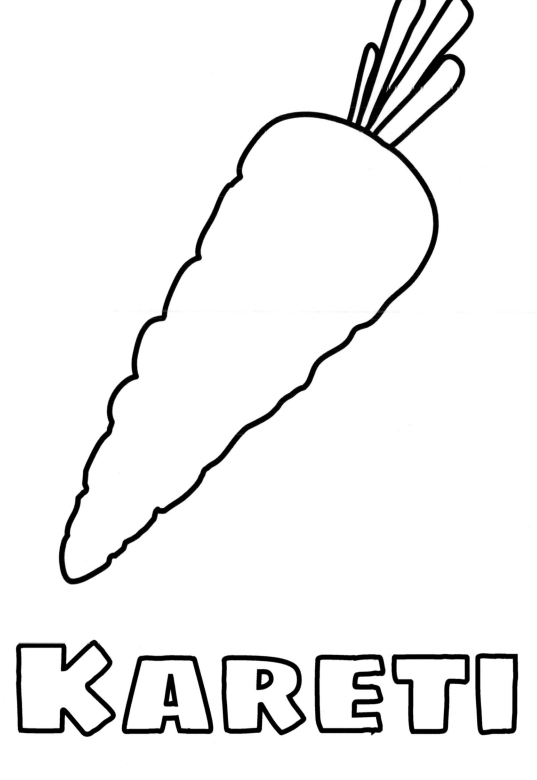

KARETI
CARROT

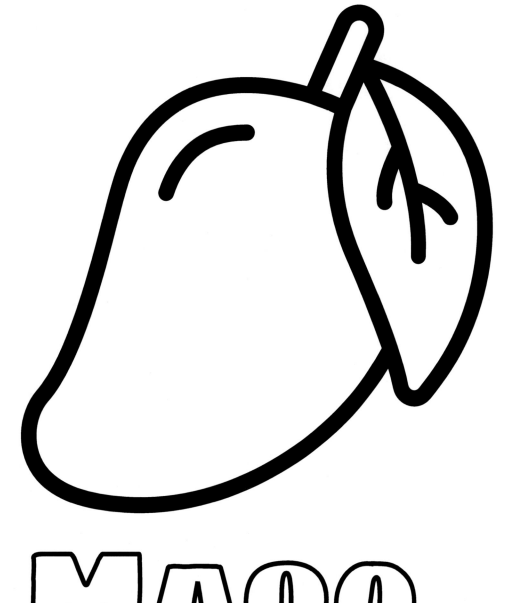

MAQO
MANGO

TOMATA

TOMATO

MOLI LEMON

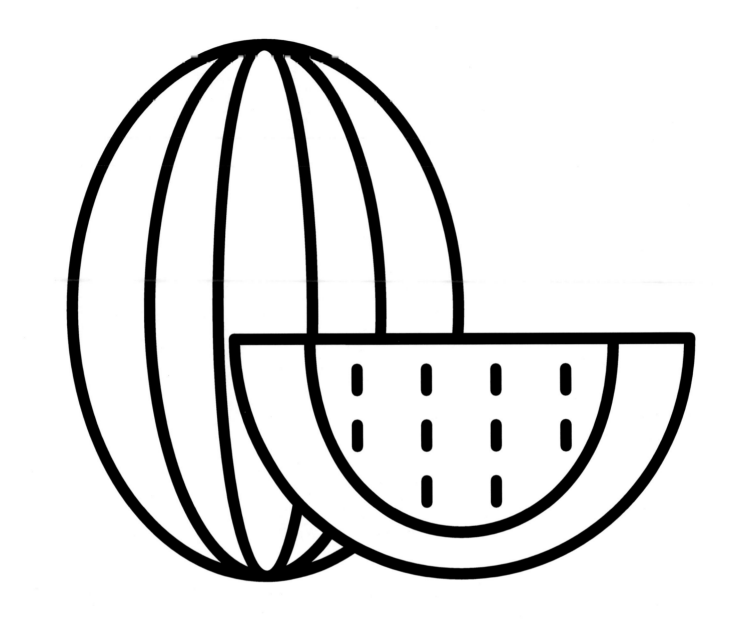

MELENI
WATERMELON

PAINAPIU
PINEAPPLE

W i

STARFRUIT

Ga

DUCK

Toa
CHICKEN

Bulumakau
COW

Vuwaka
PIG

Ose

HORSE

Me
GOAT

Lulu
OWL

Koli

DOG

Oni

BEE

Boto
FROG

Vunikau
TREE

VINAKA VAKALEVU

NI SA MOCE

GOODBYE

RO IVA'S CREATIONS

Made in United States
Orlando, FL
20 June 2023

34341669R00018